Sarah Elliott

Bible Rhymes, for Children

Sarah Elliott

Bible Rhymes, for Children

ISBN/EAN: 9783337171957

Printed in Europe, USA, Canada, Australia, Japan

Cover: Foto ©Lupo / pixelio.de

More available books at **www.hansebooks.com**

BIBLE RHYMES,

— FOR —

CHILDREN.

ILLUSTRATED.

SARAH ELLIOTT,
AUTHOR AND PROPRIETOR.

WILLIAMSPORT, PA.

1888.

PREFACE.

THE author of this little volume, during a protracted illness which unfitted her for her usual household duties, devoted much of her time to instructing an invalid child in the knowledge of the Bible; which instruction, both in character and manner, she also committed to writing;—not however with the view of ever having it published, but merely as a pleasant and profitable means of whiling away the time. But afterwards,—perhaps while reflecting on the deep interest she had awakened in the bosom of her own child in the great and gracious truths of the Word of God,—in obedience to the promptings of a love for souls, a love that refused to be circumscribed by the narrow limits of her own household, she concluded to send it forth in its present form, believing that any effort, however imperfect, to make the Holy Scriptures interesting to the young, God would be pleased to accompany and bless with his own Holy Spirit.

The work in language is especially suited to the youthful mind; and in matter is well calculated to arrest thought, impart instruction, produce conviction, and lead to Christ; and our prayer is that it may accomplish all this;—

> That the little messenger may forth to the world away
> And many little folks lead of the Book of books to say,
> Precious treasure by our Heavenly Father given,
> Brightly beams thy light to guide us home to heaven.

*

CHRIST BLESSES CHILDREN.

Bible Rhymes.

IN Genesis we read
How God had there decreed
To give this world a birth
By creating Heaven and Earth.
For day he made the light,
The darkness he called night,
The firmament, for the heavens bright;
The earth, the land so dry;
Waters he called the seas,
And said, for the fishes they shall be;
But the earth brought forth the trees,
The herbs and grass we see,
And cattle of every degree.
Then in his own image he created man,
And gave dominion over sea and land.
Every fowl of the air,
And every beast of the field was there,
That Adam might for them a name proclaim.
Then on the seventh day a rest.
God saw that all was good—the Sabbath blessed.
In this God has set us an example; beware
How we order our work, and observe it with care.
How nice this provision, how necessary for the body of
    man.
God who is merciful, did this understand.
Then we read of the beautiful Garden of Eden,
And in it were shrubs and trees that were pleasant to see;
And they bore fruit that was sweet and good to eat.
In the midst was the tree of life, and of knowledge, too,
Of good and evil, of which they were forbidden it's true;

For if they did eat they should surely die.
This command was given to Adam and wife—
This wife whom God had made for a partner for life;
A rib taken from Adam's side;
A helpmate that should by him ever abide.
In this beautiful garden bed a river of water parted into
    four heads,—
Pison, Gihon, Hiddekel and Euphrates.
Now, the subtle serpent of the field
Coaxed mother Eve to yield,
And with a sinful lie,
Said, ''Thou shalt not surely die.''
    But Satan is the father of all lies.
Flatly contradicting the assertion of God,
    To make Eve believe she is immortal he tries.
    This is the first precept God gave to man,
And as a test of his obedience—
    To obey or resist,—as he will he can.
The forbidding of this one thing had God not an abso-
    lute right to say?
And was not Adam and Eve bound to obey?
But she tasted of the fruit, and saw that it was good.
    Then gave to Adam the same;
But when God spoke she was ashamed,
    And on Satan put all the blame.
Now, this yielding to Satan's call,
Has caused man's shameful fall, alas! to all.
And since man did disobey,
He is dying, dying every day.
Therefore God sent them out of the garden, and said,
By the sweat of thy brow shalt thou earn thy bread;
And lo! over all the land shall the thorn and the thistle
    grow,
And thou shalt labor, and toil, and sow.
Ere long Cain and Abel were born,—Abel a keeper of
    sheep,
But Cain the ground did sow and reap.
                    God wanted them to offer a sacrifice;
But he who seeth the secret of the heart,
Saw in Cain's offer that faith had no part.
Jealous, he became angry and killed his brother;
But the voice of Abel's blood cried from the ground to
    God.

Cain's punishment he thought was more than he could
    stand,—   .
A fugitive and a vagabond all his days in the land.
To alleviate Adam and Eve's affliction, another son was
    given.
Seth would take their place,
Who proved to be a child of grace.

And now we will leave the descendants of mankind
Until we come down to good old Enoch's time;
Who, for his distinguished piety, was translated to the
    heavenly mansions,
Without passing through that great valley which death
    sanctions.
He was the father of Methuselah, the oldest man—
Nine hundred and sixty-nine was his alloted span.

———

NOW let us read: on account of the great depravity of
    the human race,
God sent a flood to destroy all on the earth's face.
But to Noah, a just man who walked with God, direc-
    tions he gave
How him and all his family in an ark he would save.
Then for forty days and nights the rain did fall.
The gloomy aspect caused the whole world to appall;
And not until every living thing had perished from off
    the land
Did God cause the ark on Mt. Ararat to stand.
When, lo! God showed them the beautiful rainbow,—
A token of the covenant between God and us, you know.
Now Noah was to start anew in the land,
With his three sons, Shem, Japheth and Ham;
But then, like now, they made a great mistake
By extracting the juice from out the grape.
Poor old Noah was not used to wine,
And it caused him to sin for a time.
                          As time rolled on,
These aspiring mortals could not see why
They should not build a Babylon high.
But God defeated their ambitious freak
By causing them in different tongues to speak.

Now we'll quit the genealogy of Noah's descendants to
 a time
When a universal depravity displayed itself in all man-
 kind.
         In consequence of this,
Terah, the father of Abraham, resolved to leave this
 wicked land,
And with his family, to go into the Canaan land.
But ere long we read of the Canaanites at war,
And Lot, Abraham's nephew, a captive taken sure.
Abraham to his rescue came with his armed servants,
 three hundred and eighteen.
After the victory, Melchizedek, king of Salem, came,
Blessed Abraham, and thanked God for the success given.
God was Abraham's shield in war, and exceeding great
 reward.
And now he has the promise of a son—not Ishmael, who
 from the bond-woman came—
But Isaac, who afterwards, to try Abraham's faith, was
 to be offered as a sacrifice.
   But his faith taught him to say,
   "Yea, I will obey,
   Though my son I must slay."
And when ready to kill him, with knife in hand,
God was brief, and saved him with a quick command;
And instead of his son, there appeared a ram.

     ———

THEN we read of the destruction of Sodom and Go-
 morah on account of sin;.
Not having ten righteous persons within,—
Only Lot, his wife and daughters.
But his poor wife would halt and look back;
Therefore she became a pillar of salt, or salt sack.
When Abraham grew old and knew he was not long for
 this life,
He felt anxious to have Isaac married to a good wife.
He therefore sent Eliezer, his trusty servant, back to his
 native land,
To choose for him some fair maiden's hand.
Beseeching God to direct him aright,
The beautiful Rebekah soon came in sight.

ABRAHAMS SACRIFICE.

GEN. CH. XXII. V. 12.

THE LORD'S COMMANDS SHOULD BE OBEYED
AND ALL HIS WILL ON EARTH BE DONE,
E'EN IF THE SACRIFICE BE MADE
OF A BELOVED AND ONLY SON.

She and her family treated him polite; then soon after
He told her he wished her to marry his young master.
And the young lady was willing to obey,
And so left her kindred without delay;
Perhaps God's kind angels whispered what she should
    say.
And Isaac met her and took her to his departed mother's
    tent,
And was married, was happy and content.
To them was given the great joy
Of being the parents of the first twin boys.
Alas! they had their sorrow too,
For as they to manhood grew,
Esau, for a dish of savory meat,
His birthright gave to Jacob so discreet,
Who afterwards, to obtain the blessing, did cheat;—
Made his poor old blind father believe Esau with veni-
    son was there,
By his mother helping him to cover his hands with goat's
    hair.
And now, for fear of Esau, he must leave his home;
And while wandering in a certain place, the night came
    on.
He lay down, solitary and alone,
Using for a pillow a stone.
While there he had that wonderful dream;
The ladder upon which angels were ascending and de-
    scending was seen.
And when he awoke he said, "How dreadful is this
    place."
And to him it proved a place of grace.
Then journeying, on he came to his uncle's home.
Tired and weary, he will no longer roam.
While stopping there,
He learns to love his cousin Rachel fair,
    And for her he serves his uncle seven years;
But when that time had come,
He gave him Leah, an older one.
And then he served another seven,
Until Rachel, the one he loved, was given.
And now it seemed he homesick grew,
For he took his family, and his property too,
Back to the country where his father still lived,

Who was now an hundred and four score years.
God appeared to Jacob whilst on his way,
And this is what to him he did say:
"Thy name shall no longer be Jacob, but Israel."
And then we read of his youngest son Benjamin being
born;
And his beloved Rachel dies and Israel mourns.
  Yes, Rachel dies and leaves her darling boys, Joseph
  and Benjamin.
They are young to lose their mother.
Perhaps for that reason, if for no other,
  Joseph was given the coat of many colors.
Which caused among his older brothers so much envy
  and strife,
And but for God's providence would have cost him his
  life.
Whilst we read of him telling his wonderful dream,—
How his sheaf stood up and theirs bowed to him.
His ten older brothers hate him, it is plainly seen;
And now, when they are tending their sheep in the pas-
  tures green,
Their father sends Joseph to see how they fare.
They make up their minds to murder him right there.
But Reuben, one of the best,
Not quite so sinful as the rest,
Said, Let us shed no blood, but throw him into a pit.
It harmed him not, for there was no water in it.
They took from him his spotted coat,
And sprinkled it with the blood of a goat.
And now they sit down to eat their meal,
Thinking how from their father their sin they'd conceal.
And behold! while sitting there, a band of Ishmaelites
  were passing by, equipped
With spices and myrrh, for the land of Egypt.
And they took him out and sold him to them for twenty
  pieces of silver.
And those men sold him to Potipher, one of Pharaoh's
  officers;
And the wicked brothers went home and said, This coat
  have we found.
And Jacob said, It is my son's, by some wild beast he
  has been devoured and torn.
      " With furious hands, he spreads

The scorching ashes on his graceful head,
His purple garments, and his golden hairs.
Those he deforms with dust, and these with tears." *Pope.*
But the Lord is with Joseph; he prospers and is made
    overseer in his master's house,
Until wicked ones lie about him, and accuse him of sin.
Then he is taken and cast into prison; and now it seems
That Joseph still has power to interpret dreams;
And when Pharaoh, for some petty sin, has his butler
    and baker put into prison,
One morn they were sad, it seems,
For the night before they both had dreams.
But there was no one to interpret and tell what they
    mean, until Joseph said,
One was to be restored to his place, and the other to lose
    his head.
He also said to the one that was to be restored,
Remember me in kindness to Pharaoh, thy gracious
    Lord.
But two whole years had passed,
When the ungrateful man had reason to think of him at
    last;
For Pharaoh now had dreams: the first was seven fat
    cows in a group,
And seven thin ones came along and ate them up.
Then seven good ears of corn
Were eaten by seven lean ones, and made to mourn.
But there was no one to tell him what his dreams meant,
Until the butler told him of Joseph, who for him was
    sent.
And Joseph said, the seven good meant years of plenty,
But the seven bad ones meant years of scarcity.
Then the king gave Joseph of money a great sum,
To build barns and fill them, for a famine would come.
Now, it was twenty years since he was sold a slave from
    his home,
    When his brothers from Asia were sent to buy corn.
Alas for them! his time has come,
    When they bow to him, as their sheaves in his dream
    had done.
And now their sin will find them out,
And to this day they are talked about.
Joseph speaks roughly to them, and will keep the tenth
    one,

Until they with their younger brother, Benjamin, come.
But Jacob, their father, refuses, being filled with fear,
Until the famine grew too severe.
When they came again to the place, they were treated
    good—
With a dinner prepared of delicious food.
Then their sacks were filled again,
Full and plenty, with golden grain.
But the silver cup was secretly placed in Benjamin's
    sack,
And when they were searched, they were soon brought
    back.
Joseph's time to reveal his secret now has come,
And he freely forgave them for the sin they had done.
And now they return to their father again.
To him in humility they have to explain.
Jacob, encouraged, went down into Egypt,
And when he met Joseph, in tenderness on his neck
    he wept.
Joseph introduced him to his royal master, Pharaoh,
    Who, in kindness, asked him his age;
And in Genesis forty-seven and nine you may find what
    he says
    Of his and his father's pilgrimage.
Then tranquil, happy and calm,
He settles down and lives in the Egyptian land.
And when he felt that death was nigh, he said,
Tell Joseph; and Joseph hastened to his dying bed,
And there received a blessing on his head.
And Joseph brought with him Ephraim and Manasseh,
    his two little boys.
Crossing his hands upon their heads, they his blessing
    enjoy;
But by crossing his hands, declaring the younger the
    greater boy.
Now, all his sons assemble around his bed that day
To hear what their dying father has to say;
And with his expiring breath,
The greatest is what he to Judah saith:
That the sceptre should not from him depart,
Nor a law-giver from between his feet until Shiloh come.
And now, in hope of this Saviour, Jacob is ready to say,
    "Thy will be done."

JACOB BLESSES EPHRAIM AND MANASSEH.
(GEN. CH. XXVIII. V. 6.)

NOT ALWAYS THOSE WHOSE RIGHT OF BIRTH
    WOULD SEEM TO MAKE THEIR BLESSING SURE,
ARE CHOSEN BY GOD, BUT THEY OF WORTH,
    WHOSE LIVES ARE HUMBLE, MEEK, AND PURE.

He gathered his feet into his bed,
And by faith, on Jesus' bosom reclines his head.
Like good old Simeon, he is ready to say from his heart,
I have seen thy salvation, let thy servant in peace depart.
After Joseph closed the eyes of his father and wept over
    him,
He fulfilled his promise, and buried him
In the cave of Machpelah, with his fathers, Isaac and
    Abraham.
Joseph's brothers, now that their father is no more,
A consultation held, a message sent their pardon to im-
    plore.
When Joseph read their message, he sent and had them
    all brought near,
And before he dismissed them, he removed their un-
    founded fear.
Now, fifty-four years after his father's death,
And after a life of faithfulness, death approaches,
And with a promise that his remains shall be carried into
    the Canaan land,
He, too, passes away, as did his fathers, to meet the heav-
    enly band.

NOW, the children of Israel had increased
    Until there was a great number, and the land
      was filled with his descendants;
And the new king who ruled over Egypt said:
Behold! the children of Israel are more than we,
And if there should be war, we would be whipped, I can
    plainly see.
So he set over them task-masters, who afflicted them
    with burdens great,
And made their lives bitter, all for this wicked king's
    sake.
They served in bondage, and with rigor, too;
But the more they were afflicted, the more they increased
    and grew;
Until at last, by the king's command, they every baby-
    boy,
Of the house of Levi, into the river throw.
    And now a lovely babe was born,

And for three months by his mother hid,
    For fear she, too, for her babe would have to mourn.
And when she no longer the babe could hide,
She put him in the basket of bullrushes by the river's
    side.
His little sister stood afar off to wait
And see what might be her little brother's fate.
Now Pharaoh's daughter, with her maidens, came to
    wash by the river side,
And they soon, among the bushes, the little ark espied.
And when they opened the basket, the child did weep,
And the king's daughter had compassion, and said, him
    for my own will I keep.
And Miriam, his sister, said, shall I find you a nurse?
And she hastened and brought their own mother, of
    course.
This to Moses' mother was a great privilege, again
Her own little son to care for and train.
And she impressed him with the burdens and wrongs of
    his people;
And when he was grown, he killed an Egyptian, who
    was smiting a Hebrew.
Soon after, he has reason to believe, his sin was known.
Not feeling safe, he flees from his native home,
And he dwelt in the land of Midian,
For none knew there of his wrong.
There he met and married his wife, Zipporah.
Moses, like Isaac and Jacob, the Bible tells,
Met their wives first at a well.
Now the children of Israel were groaning, by reason of
    their bondage severe,
And God remembered his covenant with them and heard
    their cry.
And the angel of the Lord appeared unto Moses in a
    burning bush,
And said, I have seen the affliction of my people—have
    come to deliver them.
Come, now, I will send thee unto Pharaoh, and without
    money
Thou shalt bring them unto a land flowing with milk
    and honey.
                        But Moses answered and said,
Who am I that I should unto Pharaoh go?

MOSES FOUND.

EXOD. CHAP. II.

THY CHILD NOW RESCUED FROM A GRAVE,
OF WATERS, MY EGYPTIAN MAID,
SHALL, ONE DAY ISRAEL'S PEOPLE SAVE,
AND BRING THEM TO THE PROMISED LAND.

And who shall I say hath sent me to do so?
God answered,
Tell them I AM, and that I have given this command;
And to prove it,
The Lord a rod turned into a serpent in Moses' hand.
This to Moses now was plain,
That when he caught it by the tail
It turned into a rod again.
Then the Lord said, Put thy hand into thy bosom,
And when he drew it out, it was white as snow;
But when he was told to pull it out the second time,
The flesh aright again did grow.
But Moses now tells God that he is afraid he is not elo-
quent enough.
This displeased God, that Moses should question so
much.
And God said,
Aaron, thy brother, a spokesman, then, shall be,
To tell what Moses from God did hear and see.
And now we read how
God sent them before Pharaoh with this command,
Let the Israelites go into the promised land.
But Pharaoh's heart was hard,
And with these poor slaves he lived content,
Until ten great plagues unto him God sent.
The first was where Aaron with his rod smote the river
Nile,
And the water all turned into blood for a while.
Then again he stretched forth his rod,
And behold the land was covered with the frog.
Then the king promised Moses to let him go with his
Israelite band,
If he would pray God to take this frog nuisance from
the land.
But his heart grew hard again, and he said, no.
He broke his promise, and would not let the Hebrews go.
And then God turned the dust into lice,
. And a bite from those many insects wasn't very nice.
Then the next was a great swarm of flies;
But they, too, were removed by another of Pharaoh's
lies.
Now, when Pharaoh's heart grew hard, and he refused
again,

The plague was a disease that killed all their cattle on
 the plains.
Then next, frightful boils on their bodies they could see,
Something that looked like the black leprosy.
Then a terrible hail storm, and fire-balls, which ran
 along the ground,
Killing all the trees and animals, except the Hebrew's;
 they were safe and sound.
Then wicked Pharaoh was frightened, and said they
 should go;
But when the hail stopped, he again told them no.
And now the locust was sent—if you read you will see—
Which destroyed every blade of grass and every green
 tree.
Then the plague of darkness—yes, darkness everyhere;
No sun, moon nor star was to be seen there.
And in that terrible plight, just about midnight,
The death angel in every family the first born did smite,
And in a moment's time there was terror in all the land.
Pharaoh himself was in agony by the bed of his oldest
 child in death's hand.
But the Hebrews, whose door-posts were sprinkled with
 the blood of a lamb,
Escaped all these plagues by obeying God's command.
Then Pharaoh yielded, and told Moses to leave with his
 Hebrew band,—
To make haste, and get away from the Egyptian land.
And now the forty years' journey of the Hebrews began,
With two and a half million of souls, for the Canaan
 land.
God placed a pillar of cloud for them to follow by day,
And a pillar of fire by night, to lead them on their way.
But in less than three days' march, hear what Pharaoh
 has to say:
He was sorry he allowed those good workmen to get
 away;
So with his chariots and horsemen he would pursue and
 drive them back without delay.
Now, in front of the poor Israelites was the red sea,
But now, in their great trouble, they went to God on
 bended knee.
Then the wind blew fiercely, pressed back the waters of
 the sea,

And the Hebrew host walked on dry land and crossed
over easily.
Now, Pharaoh and his army thought they could do the
same,
When the waters rushed upon them, and every one was
slain.
And in the morning the Israelites saw their dead bodies
washed along the shore.
Perhaps some would think they would never doubt God's
goodness any more.
But when they had eaten up all their food,
They were hungry, and said,
To have stayed with Pharaoh would have been good.
But Moses, who on God cast all his care,
Found in the morning a substitute was there.
Something white like snow was on the ground,
And when the hungry children tasted, it was good they
found.
So they were satisfied for dinner—
Yes, and for supper, too;
And the rest melted away.
What they should have to-morrow God knew.
For Moses told them not keep it over night;
Except on the sixth day, which they should with the
seventh unite.
And for forty long years those Israelites lived on the food,
Which they called manna, and always found it good.
And now we read of the first battle the Israelites had to
fight.
It was with a people called the Amalekites.
Now Moses held up his hands, and Israel prevailed;
And with Aaron and Hur's help Joshua with the sword
them assailed.

———

NOW let us read where God called Moses to top of
Mount Sinai,
And there made known the ten commandments for Israel;
yes, and for you and me.
God spoke through Moses to this people, and said, see,
I have brought you out of the land of Egypt,

And from the house of bondage made you free.
The first command is, "Thou shalt have no other Gods
    before me."
This, dear children, was intended for the whole world,
    you see.
The second is, we are not to make a graven image or
    likeness of anything
That is in heaven or on earth, neither in the waters, for
    to bow to them is a great sin.
The third is, "Thou shalt not take the name of God in
    vain."
For God will not hold us guiltless;—this to us the Bible
    has made plain.
The fourth is, "Remember the Sabbath day."
That means, we shall neither work nor play;
For in six days God created all, and rested on the Sab-
    bath day.
Now, we that love him, must this command obey,
And all within our household and gates their works must
    stay.
Now, the fifth is, "Honor thy father and thy mother,
That thy days may be long," and then
We may live the alloted time—three score years and ten.
    The sixth command is, "Thou shalt not kill."
A solemn truth to know that
    There are wicked ones who have and will.
And can it be, when they know that the wages of sin is
    death, for that is plain;
For their works do follow them, as they did the first
    murderer Cain.
The next command is the seventh: "Thou shalt not
    commit adultery;
And by God's grace, we from that sin may all be free.
And then the eighth, "Thou shalt not steal;"
But to this temptation how many yield.
    We have the promise of bread and water for our food,
And the lilies are clothed,
    And so shall we be, if we trust in God and be good.
The ninth is, not to bear false witness,
For that is a lie, it is clearly seen,
And if it were not wicked, it would be low and mean.
A falsehood cost Ananias his life—
Not only his, but that of his poor wicked wife.

The truth is, what is thy neighbor's thou shalt not covet,
But in whatsoever state we are therewith to be content,
    and live above it,
And this is God's great command,
To believe on the name of His Son, for if we believe
    not we shall be damned,
For he that despised Moses' law died without mercy,
How much sorer punishment, he who hath trodden un-
    der foot His Son, you see.
Now Moses was forty days in the mount with God alone;
It was there he received the ten commandments written
    on stone;
And whilst he was absent the Hebrews persuaded Aaron
    to make the golden calf,
And around this idol they prayed, sang, danced and
    laughed;
But God was angry, and sent Moses back, and then
The calf was burnt, and of those idolaters there were
    slain three thousand men.
After this they built a tabernacle or movable tent,
A church into which when they wanted to worship they
    went.
And when their journey was nearly o'er, the road was
    rough, and they complain,
And God was angry and had to punish them again,
By sending thousands of snakes, whose bite would have
    killed every soul;
But God told Moses to make a serpent, and put it on a
    pole,
And, a look at this serpent would cure and make them
    whole,
And how anxiously they looked, in the bible we are told.
Now, as Moses lifted up the serpent of brass on a pole,
So was the Son of Man lifted on the cross, and a look
    will save your and my soul.

NOW Balaam, a prophet, by a king was sent to come and curse the Israelites.

Starting on an ass, an angel will not let them pass; the beast talks, and Balaam's in a plight.

Now, Moses before he dies, writes a song setting forth the mercies of our God,

Telling them to command their children to observe all the words of the law.

And the Lord spake unto Moses that selfsame day and said,

Get thee up unto Mt. Nebo, and behold the lovely Cananan bed.

Moses was only allowed to look into the fair Canaan land,

On account of getting angry and striking the rock with the rod in his hand.

God had told him only to speak or command,

And the water would have come to the thirsty land.

But all have sinned, and will, who enter Paradise,—

In thought, word and deed, we sin,—

Moses by passion, Job by impatience, and Peter by cowardice.

God alone can record the number of our sins.

Moses was upright and sincere,

Having all the Christian graces in some measure whilst here;

And on top of Pisgah he died, and was buried there;

But to this day no one of his sepulchre knoweth where.

Now, to prevent any dispute, after Moses would be taken away from their sight,

Moses laid his hands upon Joshua in the presence of the people, to be a leader of the Israelites.

The first command God gave to Joshua was, to lead them over the river Jordan.

Joshua sends two spies to take a view of the strength and situation of Jericho.

Meantime the king hears of them being concealed in the house of one whose name is Rahab,

And for this kind act she afterwards rejoiced and was glad.

For whatsoever we sow, that shall we reap, and Rahab for her kindness to the spies,

Lives, and her household, whilst all others in Jericho die.

Now the Israelites were smitten at Ai, and Joshua rent
    his clothes and fell to the earth upon his face,
But the Lord said, get thee up, Israel hath sinned and
    stolen some accursed thing from this place.
Then Achan answered and said, I coveted and stole of
    their silver and gold,
So he was stoned to death and burnt, both he and all
    that he owned, we are told,
And the Lord said unto Joshua, fear not, neither be thou
    dismayed,
And all that fell that day were twelve thousand, even all
    the men of the city of Ai.
Then Joshua built an altar unto the Lord, and wrote
    upon the stones a copy of the law, as Moses had done,
And, as Joshua those laws obeyed, divers kings and
    countries by him were overcome.
Then, after many years, when Joshua felt that he was
    growing old,
He to the Israelites spoke, and God's benefits, even from
    Abraham to them, he told,
And exhorted them to obey God in sincerity and truth.
As for himself and his household, they would serve and
    obey both.
Not long after this he dies, being an hundred and ten,
And was buried in the beautiful mount Ephraim.
Now Ehud, who subdued the Moabites, appears,
And after subduing them, the Israelites have rest four-
    score years.
Then the children of Israel again did evil in God's sight,
Deborah, a prophetess, by the aid of the Lord helped
    them out of this plight,
And then Deborah sings a song of praise,
And the land has rest another forty years.
After Deborah's day, we read of Gideon's reign, his chil-
    dren and his death,
And then of Jotham's parable, and what he of the trees
    saith,
Then the Sheckemites, and the Amalekites, the Israel-
    ites again oppressed,
For now again they had forsaken God, and felt that by
    Him they were no longer blessed.
And now the Israelites choose Jephthah for their captain
    to fight the Amorites.

This Jephthah vowed a vow, that if he gained the vic-
tory,
He would sacrifice of his house the first that came in
sight.
Behold when he comes nigh his home, his beautiful
daughter, an only child,
Comes out to meet him, with timbrels and dances in joy
so wild;
Alas, what he has vowed to the Lord that he now must
do,
And after two months his beautiful daughter he sacri-
ficed.
Then we read of the Ephraimites that were slain,
Then of Manoah, and from him Samson came,
Samson so strong that he slew a lion as easy as if it had
been something tame.
After a time he returned, and seeing the lion's carcass,
his riddle he tells,
And had it not been for his bad wife, they could not
have guessed, and all would have been well.
The riddle was—Out of the eater came forth meat,
And out of the strong came forth sweet.
And the Philistines said, what is sweeter than honey,
And what is stronger than a lion, and now he knows
that his wife was a cheat.
  Samson is angry now, and by his next action he shows
it plain,
For he caught three hundred foxes, and to them he tied
fire brands,
  Then let them into their fields of grain.
Then they caught him and bound him with great strong
bands.
But the Lord came mightily upon him, and he broke
them loose from off his hands.
It was then, with the jaw-bone of an ass, that he slew a
thousand men.
But now he does another very foolish thing:
He again tells a woman that his strength is in his hair.
And now those wicked people take him and put out his
eyes.
Howbeit, his hair again did grow, and God, who is mer-
ciful, heard his cries.

And when the Philistines were merry, they called for
    Samson, for they wanted some sport.
But Samson called for strength and vengeance, and he
    was answered by the Lord;
And he said to a lad, lead me by the hand;
Suffer me to feel the pillars upon which this house stands.
And he bowed himself with all his might, and took hold
    of the pillars on either side,
And with all this people he was crushed, and with them
    he died.
And after Samson we read of the desolation of the Ben-
    jamites, and their destruction, too,
For the Israelites had great battles with them until they
    were subdued.

———

AND now we come to the beautiful book of Ruth
    And all who are acquainted with the Bible have read
    this sweet story from their youth;
How there was a famine in Bethlehem of Judea.
And now Elimelech, with his wife Naomi and two sons,
    went to the country of Moab.
The sons marry Orpha and Ruth, but the father and sons
    die, and Naomi no longer will make this her abode.
Now, when she is ready to depart, she kisses her daugh-
    ters-in-law, and bade them go to their mother's
    home.
Orpha obeyed, but Ruth said, entreat me not to leave
    thee, for where thou goest, there am I willing with
    thee to roam.
And when their journey is over, and they are back to
    Naomi's native home and kinsman,
They welcome her with an idle curiosity, seeing her
    daughter-in-law is a lovely woman.
But their welcoming is without much love, charity or
    liberality.
Ruth, who has forsaken all for Naomi and Naomi's God,
    is not frightened at poverty;
And as the custom of that country allowed the poor what
    corn they might find after the reaper,
This was comforting to Ruth, and she arose,

And the Gracious Being who guides our steps, directed
 Ruth to the field of Boaz.
The first words that greet her ears is a devout prayer,
 "May the Lord be with thee."
Thus was the fidelity of Ruth rewarded, for she became
 the wife of this wealthy man.
To her was given the honor of being to David a great
 grandmother.
And from David came the Redeemer, the Saviour of
 mankind, and greater than He there is no other.

————

AFTER the book of Ruth, we read of Samuel,
 Who was given to Hannah, his mother, in answer
  to prayer,
And Elkanah, his father, with his family, went up out
 of the city yearly
To sacrifice unto the Lord, and the priests were there.
Therefore, when Samuel was old enough, they took him
 up, and on account of the answer to his mother's
 prayer
They gave him to the Lord.
And the child ministered unto the Lord before Eli the
 priest.
But Eli's sons did not love nor serve their father's God.
Now Eli heard of his son's sins, and reproved them
 gently, but they heeded him not; he ought to have
 been more severe,
To train up a child in the way he should go,
And when he is old he will not depart from it,—the Bible
 makes this verse clear.
Now the child Samuel grew, and was in favor with both
 God and man,
And every year when his mother came up to sacrifice,
 she brought him a little coat, made by her own
 hands,
And it came to pass after a time that Eli had lain down,
 for he was now old and almost blind.
Samuel too had lain down to sleep, but he hears some
 one call in a short time;
Of course he thought Eli had spoken to him, and ran
 in to see what he had said,

Ruth.

But the aged man told him he had not called him, and
    that he should go back to bed;

But when it was repeated the second, yes the third time,
    Eli told him then to say, Speak, Lord, for thy ser-
    vant heareth,

Then was revealed to Samuel, the destruction of Eli's
    sons, in a vision to him it all appeareth;

And Eli called Samuel, and wanted to know all,

And said, it is the Lord, let him do what seemeth good.

Samuel felt sorry, but explained it all,

How his sons made themselves vile, and he restrained
    them not, and Eli understood.

Now the Philistines and Israelites have war again,

And Eli's two sons, Hophni and Phineas are both slain,

And when a messenger came, and told Eli of their death,
    and that the ark was taken, he fell backwards and
    died.

After this there was deadly destruction among the Phil-
    istines, and the hand of God was heavy upon them;

And after having the ark seven months, they called the
    priests and were ready to return it to them.

Now Samuel spoke to the house of Israel, beseeching
    them to serve the Lord in peace;

And the Israelites, now that they had discomfited the
    Philistines, wanted Samuel to cry unto the Lord,
    and not cease.

Then Samuel judged Israel all the days of his life,

And when he was old, he wanted his sons made judges
    over them; but then again there was strife;

And they answered him, Thy sons walk not in thy ways,
    now make us a king.

And Samuel prayed unto the Lord, and the Lord said,
    Give them a king,

But they have rejected me by doing this thing.

Now there was a handsome young man whose name was
    Saul, and he was a son of a Benjamite,

And Saul's father's asses were lost, and he sent Saul and
    a servant to seek them, for they had wandered out
    of sight.

And they passed through Ephraim, Shalisha, Shalim,
    and came to the land of Zuph;

Then Saul said to the servant, we will return, or father
    will take thought of us,—we have hunted enough.

But the servant answered, in this city there is an honorable man of God, peradventure he can show us which way to steer;

And Saul said, behold we have no present to give, but the servant answered, I have a fourth part of a sheckel; come, we will go to the seer.

And as they went up into the city they inquired of some young maidens at a well.

Get you up, for about this time ye shall find him, for he doth bless the sacrifice; this is what to them the young maidens tell.

Now, the Lord had told Samuel that "to-morrow about this time I will send thee a man;"

And when Samuel saw Saul he said, "Go up into the high place," for Samuel the Lord did understand.

So Samuel took a vial of oil, and poured it upon his head; and now Saul is their anointed king.

And the people sang, long live the king!

But Saul's reign was a wicked one, and before it was over they ceased to sing;

And the Lord rejected Saul for his disobedience,

And Samuel mourns; but the Lord said, fill thine horn with oil and go to Jesse, the Bethlehemite.

And he went and called Jesse and his sons to a sacrifice.

Then seven of his sons passed by; but Samuel said, the right one is not in sight.

And samuel said, are these all thy children?

But Jesse answered, there is one younger, a shepherd boy.

And Jesse sent and brought in his ruddy, goodly and beautiful boy,

Who had perhaps, in his hands, a harp, his only toy.

And Samuel arose and anointed him; and as Saul, after he had been anointed, returned to his field,

So David returned to his flock.

And as the path to the throne was to be opened by circumstances which did not yet appear,

He was still to attend to his father's stock.

Perhaps it was then he wrote—"When I consider thy heavens, the work of thy hands;

The moon and stars which thou hast ordained;

What is man, that thou art mindful of him?

And the son of man, that thou visitest him?"

And then he proclaimed: "For thou hast made him a little lower than the angels,

And hast crowned him with glory and honor.''
Now Saul's fall came, for he did not deserve to stand so
    high,
And the people wondered who should succeed him upon
    the throne.
Now, from that time the spirit of the Lord rested upon
    David, but from Saul it had departed.
Then he was melancholy, and wanted a song,
And his friends told him of David's skill;
    So he was sent for, and he came and stood before Saul.
And Saul loved him, and he became his armor-bearer,
And David took his harp and played with his hands.
    It refreshed Saul, and he was better of his gloomy
    terror.
Now the Israelites and Philistines are preparing for
    battle,
    And there went out a champion from the Philistines,
    a giant, Goliath, who stood eight feet high,
And David was sent by his father to inquire of his
    brothers' welfare.
    For they are in Saul's army, and Jesse loves as only
    those do who are bound together by a family tie.
Now, for forty days had this monster challenged Saul's
    army.
    And in this way stood affairs when David arrived at
    the camp;
And the heroic youth was curious, and wanted it all re-
    lated to him;
    But his eldest brother reproved him severely;—now,
    this was cruel after his long tramp.
But David replied in a respectful tone, what have I done?
    is there not a cause?
    I am willing to encounter Goliath, and his words were
    told to Saul;
And Saul sent for him, but when David appeared he re-
    jected him, saying,
    You are but a youth, and Saul's countenance again
    did fall.
But David, guided by the power of Omnipotence
    To remove the objection of Saul, related how he had
    rescued a lamb from a lion and bear.
David said, moreover, that the Lord, who had delivered
    him from those wild animals,

Would be with him in the battle there.
The faith of David astonished Saul, and he said, put the
    royal armor upon him,
And let him go.   But David put it off; he only wanted
    a stone and a sling.
So with a few pebbles from a brook, in his shepherd's bag,
He went forth to meet Goliath, perhaps with no more
    fear than when for Saul he played.
But when Goliath saw only a shepherd boy, he said:
"Am I a dog, that thou comest to me with staves?"
Now he is in a terrible rage; he curses David and says:
"Come, I will give thy flesh to the fowls of the air !"
He looked for victory through the sword and spear.
David trusted alone in God, saying, "This day will the
    Lord deliver thee into my hands,
And this assembly shall know that it was not by the
    sword nor spear."
Now Goliath's pride was touched to the quick,
And he hastened to crush David; but the contest ended
    very queer,
For a stone thrown from the hand of David entered into
    the giant's forehead,
Just as he threw up his haughty head and disdainfully
    laughed.
Then it was told Saul how, without sword or spear, but
    with a stone's waft,
And how with Goliath's own sword he had then cut off
    his head,
And that now the Philistines' leader being dead they
    had all fled.
Then Saul said unto David "Whose son art thou?"
For perhaps he remembered his promise or vow,
To any one who this giant should kill,
Should marry his daughter if he will.
And David answered, I am the son of Jesse;
Then Saul said, my house thy home shall be.
It was now that David learned to love Saul's son,
And he won the heart of this royal prince Jonathan.
Perhaps on account of David's great act he admired and
    loved him, too,
Even when he had heard that David was to be king
    and knew it to be true;
And several times when Saul would have killed David,

Then Jonathan apprised David of the designs, and his
    life was saved;
And when Saul and his gallant son fell in battle,
David's lamentations over Jonathan is, Oh Jonathan,
    my brother, very pleasant hast thou been unto me;
Thy love to me was wonderful, passing the love of wo-
    man.
And years afterwards he showed his kindness to Jona-
    than's son for Jonathan's sake,
And said to him, thou shalt eat bread at my table con-
    tinually, seeing thou art lame in both feet.
But David was far from being without sin,
As in Nathan's rebuke it is plainly seen,
And in the fifty-first Psalm is David's own acknowledg-
    ment:
"Have mercy upon me, Oh God." His great sin he
    feels and understands.
In the whole of this beautiful chapter he confesses his
    sin, and asks forgiveness at God's hand.
Now there was all kinds of trouble in the house of
    David,
For David, like Eli and Samuel, had wicked sons, too,
And they murdered and sinned in many ways, it is true.
Absalom, who is spoken of as a beautiful man, conspires
    to get the throne
From David his father, who to the mountain fled.
But God is with him, and David had a father's love
Even for his wicked boy, and he says to his men, deal
    gently with him for my sake.
Now when the battle was fierce, Absalom rode upon a
    mule, and the mule went under
The thick boughs of a great oak.
Then was he slain by ten young men;
And tidings were taken to David who was waiting and
    watching to know if Absalom was safe.
And when he was told, he wept, and said,
"O! my son Absalom, my son, my son Absalom,
Would to God I had died for thee; O! Absalom, my son."
And the victory was turned into mourning that day;
Afflicted for the loss of a wicked son you might say.
And Joab, a soldier, came and reproved David for his
    immoderate grief.
Then the king arose and administered justice to the
    people and sat in the gate.

And as David grew old, he said: Solomon, my son, shall
    be king in my stead,
For I have appointed him ruler over Israel and Judah;
    then to Solomon he said:
"I go the way of all the earth; be thou strong therefore,
    and show thyself a man,
And keep the charge of the Lord thy God, to walk in
    his ways and keep his commandments."
And King David died, and was buried in the city of
    David,
After reigning over Israel forty years.

———

THEN sat Solomon upon the throne of his father,
    For it was his from the Lord, it appears.
Now the Lord appeared unto Solomon in a dream,
    And said, "Ask what I shall give thee."
Then answered Solomon, "Thou hast made me king,
    O Lord,
    And I am but a little child," you see.
"I know not how to go out or come in before thy chosen
    people,
    For who is able to judge them aright?
Give therefore thy servant an understanding heart,
    That I may discern between good and evil in thy
    sight."
This request so pleased God that he gave him wisdom
    in abounding measure,
    Such as none before him had ever possessed;
And now, since he had made so excellent a choice,
    He would give him riches and honor without even
    Solomon's request.
    Ere long Solomon has a chance to display his wisdom
    by settling a quarrel between two women,
Who both claimed a living child, and both disowned one
    that had died.
    Solomon knew that the real mother would be most
    human,
When he said, bring me a sword and divide the living
    child,
    And give half to the one and half to the other.
The one said, let it be divided, but the other said, Oh,
    my Lord, give her the living child.

Then Solomon said, she is the rightful mother.
Now, God gave Solomon wisdom and understanding ex-
    ceeding much,
    Even as the sand that is on the seashore.
And he spake three thousand proverbs,
    And his songs were a thousand and more.
Then we read of the preparations for the great temple,
Which David, when he ascended the throne of Israel
    had resolved to erect.
God approved of his designs, but because he was a man
    of war, for him to build the house he did reject;
But at the same time he gave him a promise
That his son Solomon, who was directed in wisdom's
    ways, should fulfill his intentions.
And David acquiesced in the Divine will;
And to enable his son to make such a glorious display,
He himself commenced preparations by giving a thou-
    sand thousand talents of silver,
And an hundred thousand talents of gold,
And of brass and iron without weight, for there was such
    an abundance it was not told.
And David moreover gave to Solomon a pattern for the
    house of the Lord,
    And said, Arise and be doing,
And the Lord be with thee; be strong and of good cour-
    age; fear not,
    Nor be dismayed whilst the Lord's service you are
    pursuing.
    Now Hiram, king of Tyre, a friend of Solomon's,
    complied with his request.
In building this great temple they employed one hundred
    and eighty-three thousand men,
    All working in harmony and doing their best,
And everything was made ready ere it came to the place;
Neither hammer nor axe was heard whilst they were
    building at Mt. Moriah.
Now, after seven and a half years, this beautiful house
    was finished and dedicated to God;
And now let us read the beautiful prayer of Solomon's,
    as he stood before the altar of the Lord.
The Queen of Sheba heard but could not believe of Solo-
    mon's grandeur, beauty and wealth;
But when she came, she said, the half had not been told.
Nor would she believe until she had seen for herself.

But now, in the midst of all his glory and wealth, he
　　has contention and strife.
He forsook the God of his mercies by marrying an idol-
　　atrous wife.
After solemnly declaring that his people should not give
　　their daughters to the heathens.
He turns his heart away from God by taking wives from
　　the surrounding nations.
One of those wives was the daughter of Pharaoh, the
　　Egyptian king.
This itself was enough to cause him to neglect his own
　　religion and sin.
Now, when we think of Solomon, how good he was in
　　his youth,
And that, for all we know he was lost, it is a fearful and
　　solemn truth,
After even having God to answer his prayer and give
　　him his praise
For his choosing knowledge and wanting to walk in
　　wisdom's ways.
No wonder he writes this melancholy sentence, "Vanity
　　of vanities, all is vanity."
Out of Christ, he had many sorrowful days.
Solomon did not live the three score years and ten, the
　　allotted time of man.
Perhaps he lived contrary to the laws of nature, and so
　　shortened his days, as any one can.

———

AFTER Solomon's death, we read of his only son Re-
　　hoboam's wicked reign.
The tribes were now divided, and all the tribes but two
　　did Jeroboam claim.
This Jeroboam from Egypt came, and after Rehoboam's
　　reign and death,
There was Abijah's wicked reign, and Asa's good one,
　　so the Bible saith.
His heart was pure, and he worshipped the true God
　　only.
Then Jehoshaphat, his son, reigned in his stead,
And of his reign, it was good, it is said.

But of all the good and bad kings which reigned,
We can not make mention of all, it is plain;   ·
So if we speak of the noted ones, let this explain,
Some being kings of Judah and some of Israel.
We next mention Omri, and his leading the people to
    idolatry was a shame.
Now after Omri reigned, Ahab over Israel reigned, and
    he took to wife Jezebel. ·
She, the daughter of an idolatrous king, was terribly
    cruel.
Now God sent Elijah to this wicked king to say that
    there should be no dew nor rain.
Then the Lord said to Elijah, hide thyself by the brook,
    for there thou shalt be sustained.
There the ravens brought him bread and flesh in the
    morn and eve;
And from the brook his water to drink he received.
Now there was no rain and the brook dried up—the
    drought was coming, it was plain.
But God said, get thee to Zarephath, for a widow there
    shall thee sustain.
And behold when he came to the gate of the city,
    The widow was there gathering sticks,
And he called to her and said,
Give me a drink and a morsel of bread.
    But now she is in a terrible fix;
And she answered and said, I have but a handful of meal
    and a cruse of oil,
Which I was going to cook, then eat and die.
But Elijah said unto her, make me thereof a little cake
    first, and bring it unto me,
And after make for thy son and thee.
Thy barrel of meal shall not waste nor thy oil fail, for
    .thus the Lord saith.
This was certainly a remarkable trial of this woman's
    faith.
But she obeyed, and she and her house did eat many
    days,
And the meal did not waste nor the oil fail, for they did
    according to the Lord's ways.
And it came to pass, after these things, that this woman's
    son took sick and died,
And she came and told Elijah, and he said,

"Give me thy son," and he took him and laid him upon
    his own bed.
And he cried unto the Lord, and this is what he said:
"O Lord, I pray thee, let this child's soul come into him
    again."
And the Lord heard, the child revived,
And the mother was led to seek the truth, and all this
    good was obtained.

———

AT this time there lived one Naboth, who owned a
    lovely vineyard nigh to Ahab's home,
And Ahab coveted it and wished to add it to his own.
He offers to give him a better vineyard, or the worth of
    it in money.
But Naboth rejected the proposal, saying it was his
    father's, and he would not agree.
Now, the refusal of Naboth caused Ahab to be down-
    hearted, and he would eat no bread,
And Jezebel, his wife, said, "Dost thou not govern the
    kingdom?"
"Let thine heart be merry, I will give thee the vine-
    yard."
So she wrote letters in Ahab's name, proclaiming a fast
    and setting Naboth on high,
And told two wicked men, who cared not from the truth
    to depart,
To say that Naboth had blasphemed God and the king.
Then they took him and stoned him, and thus he lost
    his life,
All through the sayings and doings of Ahab's wicked
    wife.
She then said to Ahab, arise, take possession of the vine-
    yard, for Naboth is dead.
And he arose up to go down, and the word of the Lord
    came to Elijah and said,
Tell Ahab, where dogs licked the blood of Naboth shall
    dogs lick even thine.
(It is supposed by some, that at the same place where
    Naboth was stoned, Ahab's blood was licked up by
    dogs and swine.

And years afterwards, when Jehu was executing judg-
　ment upon the house of Ahab, he makes Jezebel
　dog's meat,

By causing her to be thrown from a window, and then
　trodden on by horses' feet.)

Now, in the third year, the Lord said unto Elijah, "Go
　show thyself unto Ahab, and I will send rain."

For there was a sore famine in Samaria; on account of
　the great drouth there was suffering, it is plain.

And Obadiah, the governor of Ahab's house, meets
　Elijah, it appears.

Now, Obadiah feared the Lord greatly—was zealous and
　sincere.

(We omitted Obadiah's sayings, and as he was a good
　man,·

Let us turn back a little, please, to understand.)

Now, through Obadiah, Elijah and Ahab meet,

And Elijah proposes that the prophets of Baal and him-
　self should offer a sacrifice.

They should offer theirs to their gods, and he would to
　Jehovah,

And the god who would send down fire to consume the
　sacrifice, he should rule over all.

The proposal was accepted, and in vain did the priests
　of Baal call the whole day long,

Then Elijah offers his sacrifice and prays to God, and
　fire comes down, and the people's faith in Jehovah
　is strong.

Then the people slew all the prophets of Baal that day;

For now they halt no more between two opinions, for
　hear what they say:

"The Lord he is the God, the Lord he is the God," they
　all proclaim.

Then Elijah said unto Ahab, "Get thee up, eat and
　drink, for there will now be an abundance of rain."

And Ahab told Jezebel all that Elijah had done, and
　how he had had the prophets slain.

She is terribly enraged, and sends a message to Elijah
　that by to-morrow he too should die.

When he hears this he flees to Beer-sheba, and then a
　day's journey into the wilderness.

Discouraged, he requested for himself that he might die
　as he lay under the juniper tree;

But an angel touched him and said, "Arise and eat,"
And he looked, and behold! there was a cake and a cruse
of oil at his feet.
And the angel touched him the second time and said,
"Arise and eat,"
For thy journey from Beer-sheba to Mt. Horeb for thee
is too great,
And he arose, and did eat and drink, and went forty days
and nights in the strength of that meat.
He fasted just the same length of time as Moses, and as
Christ in the wilderness did.
"And he came thither unto a cave and lodged there,"
And the Lord said, "Elijah, what doest thou here?"
And he said, "They have slain the prophets, and I only
am left.
And they seek to take my life away."
And the Lord said, "Go forth and stand upon the mount."
Perhaps in the same place where Moses had stood.
And whilst he was there, the Lord passed by, and there
was a great strong wind, but in it no good,
And after the wind an earthquake, and then a fire;
But the Lord was not in either;
But after the fire, a still small voice;
And when Elijah heard it, he wrapped his face in his
mantle,
And stood in the entrance of the cave, perhaps to re-
joice.
And the Lord said, return and anoint Jehu, for he shall
be king over Israel soon,
And Elisha anoint to be prophet in thy room.
So he departed, and found Elisha ploughing, with twelve
yoke of oxen before him;
And Elijah passed by and cast his mantle upon him.
It appears that Elisha is wealthy, but he is willing to
leave his oxen and all.
He only asked to return home to kiss and bid farewell
to his parents before obeying the Divine call.
Now, Benhadad, king of Syria,
With thirty-two other kings, besieged Samaria;
Then the king of Israel called his army, and they ar-
rayed themselves,·
And Israel was victorious;—the Syrians fled.
Then the Syrians said that the Lord was God of the hills,
but not of the valley.

And there came a man of God to the king of Israel and
    said, rally,
And God will deliver all this great multitude into thy
    hand,
And ye shall know that God is the Lord of all the land.
And the children of Israel slew of the Syrians one hun-
    dred thousand footmen in one day,
But the rest fled to the city of Aphek, and there, a wall
    falling twenty-seven thousand of the remainder did
    slay.
Now it came to pass, when Elijah was about to be taken
    up into heaven,
That he asked Elisha what he should do for him before
    he should leave him;
And Elisha said, "Let a double portion of thy spirit fall
    upon me."
And Elijah replied, "Thou hast asked a hard thing:
    nevertheless, if thou seest me when I am taken then
    shall it be."
And behold there appeared a chariot, and horses of fire,
    and parted them;
And Elisha saw it, and cried, "My father, my father;"
    and he saw him no more,
For he went up by a whirlwind into heaven.

NOW, as Elisha was going up unto Bethel, there came
    forth little children mocking him;
    And this is what they said, "Go up, thou bald head;
      go up, thou bald head."
And he turned, and looking on them, in the name of
    the Lord he cursed them;
    And there came forth two she bears out of the woods
      and tare forty-two of them until they were dead.
Now a widow of one of the prophets is oppressed by a
    merciless creditor;
And she goes to the man of God, Elisha, and tells him
    that all she has is a pot of oil in the door.
And he told her to go borrow vessels, and to fill, and she
    filled until there was not a vessel more.
Then he said, sell the oil, pay thy debt, and live thou
    and thy children as of yore.

The next miracle Elisha did, is when a father takes his
 little son out to the reapers,
 And he is taken sick and cries, oh, my head, my head.
And his father said to a lad, carry him to his mother;
 And she holds him until noon, but now he is dead.
This mother, too, hastens to the man of God, showing
 by this that she has faith in him.
But Elisha must work hard with the child,
For it is not faith alone, but the power of God that re-
 stored the child to life again.
Next we read of Naaman, who, being captain of the host
 of the king of Syria, was a great man.
But he was a leper, afflicted with a disease the most loath-
 some and humiliating in all the land.
Now, Naaman had sent out troops into the land of Israel
 To steal and take cattle, and inhabitants for slaves,
And these had stolen a little maid,
 And through her instrumentality, God this wicked
 Naaman saves.
This pious little maid had told Naaman's wife
If only her prophet were there, he might be able to save
 her master's life.
And when they told the king what she had said, he sent
 a letter and great presents to the king of Israel;
But the king was frightened, and thought that the king
 of Syria wanted to seek a quarrel.
Elisha hearing this, orders Naaman to be brought to him
 that he may know his fate.
So Naaman comes to his door with horses and chariots
 in great state;
But Elisha only sends a message, saying, "Go wash in
 Jordan seven times and be clean."
But Naaman thought such an inexpensive and simple
 mode of cure contemptible and mean,
And thought his own rivers at home as good as the wa-
 ters of Jordan, and so went away in a rage.
Then his servants called him father, and said, "Had he
 bid thee do some great thing" for the cleansing stage,
Would'st thou not have done it?" then went he down
 and dipped seven times;
Then was his flesh like a little child's;
The scurf being removed, and he, in health, with joy is
 almost wild.

Now does he acknowledge that there is none other such
a God in all the earth,

And he experienced what the Lord taught Nicodemus
about the new birth.

Now Elisha had a servant, Gehazi, who coveted the
great presents which Naaman brought, and which
Elisha refused,

And he ran after Naaman and said, "My master hath sent
me; give me I pray thee the silver and two changes
of garments," if thou choose.

And when he received it he carried it to a dark place to
conceal.

Then he came and stood before Elisha, his master, and
Elisha to him made this appeal:

"Whence comest thou," and he answered, "Thy servant went no whither."

And Elisha said, "Went not mine heart with thee?

Therefore Naaman's leprosy shall cleave unto thee."

And now we read of good reigns and of bad reigns, and
then we read that Elisha died.

Elijah and Elisha were two great men, and with them
did God's spirit ever abide.

And now again and again we read of wicked and cruel
reigns until we come to Hezekiah,

For he trusted in the Lord God of Israel, and kept Moses'
commandments as he them understood.

He broke in pieces the brazen serpents, which they were
now worshiping,

And when the king of Assyria sends Rab-shakeh unto
Hezekiah, he comes blaspheming;

And his impudent speech is without parallel, for the re-
port had now gone abroad

That the Jews placed the utmost confidence in their
God.

Now Hezekiah in his distress, sends for Isaiah the prophet, and he prays,

And the Lord sent a blast among them, which caused a
terrible sight,

The blast, or suffocating wind, slew one hundred and
eighty-five thousand in one night.

And afterwards, Hezekiah was sick unto death,

And Isaiah the prophet came to him and said,

"Set thine house in order, for thou shalt die and not
live;"

And he wept sore, and beseeched God to spare him, and
    God granted him fifteen more years,
The nation was in danger from the Assyrian army, and
    Hezekiah wanted to see them defeated, it appears.
He was the first and only man who ever was informed of
    the term of his life.
Now the king of Babylon and Hezekiah must have been
    on friendly terms, but which ended in strife,
By the king of Babylon sending his son with a letter
    and presents to congratulate Hezekiah,
For he had heard of his sickness and miraculous cure;
And Hezekiah was so pleased that he showed them all
    the precious treasures in his house—
    The gold, silver, spices and ointment.
This, on his part, was folly,
    For behold the day came by appointment
When the Babylonians took this land from them; for
    when they saw its wealth they coveted it.
But it was not in Hezekiah's day; and after fifteen years
    he slept with his fathers.
And then Manasseh, his son, reigned in his stead; but
    he was a wicked one ;
And then Amon, who also was wicked. But now we
    come
To the young monarch Josiah, a model boy,
Who, at eight years of age, began to seek after the God
    of David. This was his joy,
And to do what was right in the sight of God was his
    constant employ.
His father and grandfather were both wicked men.
Perhaps he had had the prayers of a pious mother.
The first thing he did was to repair the house of the
    Lord,
And to gather together all the idols that were scattered
    abroad.
These images, for fear they should be set up again, were
    to powder ground,
And the dust was strewed on the graves, for those who
    would touch what was near the dead were not to be
    found.
Now whilst they were repairing the house of the Lord,
    they found Moses' book of the law,
Which perhaps had been buried under the cornerstone;

This was saved, and this alone,
For Manasseh and Amon had tried to have them all destroyed.
In this book were written terrible things against the corrupters of God's word.
Then Josiah sent Hilkiah the priest unto Huldah the prophetess,
And she answered and said unto them, the Lord said thus:
"My wrath shall be kindled against this place, and shall not be quenched."
But Josiah, whose heart is tender before God,
Should not see this desolation, but be gathered unto his grave in peace.
Now not long after Josiah's death, as God had decreed,
Nebuchadnezzar, king of Babylon, came up against Jerusalem, and the city was besieged.
Ere long the inhabitants were scattered in every direction,
And those who were not captured had to flee;
The walls of Jerusalem were broken down, and thus was Judah carried away out of her own land,
Also everything of value upon which they could lay their hand.
This was four hundred and sixty-eight years after David over Jerusalem began to reign,
And five hundred and ninety years before Christ came.
Now among the young Jewish princes were four who excelled the rest,
At least they feared the Lord in this strange land the best.
Their names were Daniel, Hananiah, Mishael and Azariah.
And now their love to God is to be tested.
Nebuchadnezzar erected an image of gold for his subjects to worship, that they might be blessed,
And when these refused to bow to this image, the king is told;
He then is furious, and in great wrath,
Orders a furnace to be heated seven times hotter than usual,
And into this they were bound and cast;
But God's promise to Isaiah is here fulfilled,—

"When thou walkest through the fire thou shalt not be
    burnt, neither shall the flame kindle upon thee,"
For an angel of God appeared in the furnace,
And those young men were safe, and walked at liberty.
Then Nebuchadnezzar spoke and said,
Blessed be their God! Let no one speak
Or say anything amiss against their God, for him will
    we seek.
We have reason to believe he died in the faith,
For he praised and honored the King of Heaven, the
    Bible saith.
Now we read of his grandson Belshazzar, who now was
    king,
But he is profaning, and doing wicked things.
At a feast where a thousand of his lords were drinking
    wine,
A hand on the wall appeared writing a line.
None being able to interpret it, by the queen's request
    Daniel is called.
He explains the meaning and tells them of their fearful
    fall;
And that very night the prediction was fulfilled and the
    king slain,
And Medes and Persians took possession.
And one Darius is now made king of Babylon.
Darius, when he heard of Daniel's great wisdom,
Made him ruler over the whole realm.
Then the rulers and princes sought to find fault with
    Daniel;
And knowing that he was good and faithful, persuaded
    the king to establish this decree,
That for thirty days no one should pray save unto the
    king; and now they will see
If Daniel will obey, or if he will dare
Any longer take consolation in prayer.
Now, Daniel knew that the writing was signed; never-
    theless, on bended knee,
Three times a day, at his window praying, him could
    they see.
And Daniel knew, too, that if he prayed, his punish-
    ment would be the lions' den;
But God sent an angel to this good man,
And shut the lions' mouths, and they were as gentle as
    lambs.

Then the king arose early and came out in haste,
And when Daniel came out unhurt, he no time did waste,
But had those men brought and thrown into the lions'
den.
Then were the lions' mouths opened, and the men were
slain.

———

THE Jewish captivity lasted seventy years, when Cy-
rus, king of Persia,
Fulfills the prophecy of Jeremiah, being told perhaps by
Daniel that he was chosen before he was born for
this task.
With matchless zeal he performs his work at last.
He made a proclamation, saying that God had charged
him to build him a house at Jerusalem again.
Then he gives all that Nebuchadnezzar had taken—brass,
silver and gold,
With goods, beasts, and precious things besides, we are
told.
The number of those who returned from Babylon were
forty-two thousand, three hundred and three-score,
And the servants were seven thousand or more.
And while building the temple, the people sang and
praised the Lord.

Now we read of another eminent man, Nehemiah, who
helped to build Jerusalem's broken walls;
And so faithful were Nehemiah and his men at this work
That they did not take off their clothes, only to bathe,
for a month at a time.
Nehemiah said, "Think upon me, my God, for good,
for all is thine."
He wishes for no reward from man;
He only asks for mercy at God's hand.
So, with several thousand workmen, in fifty-two days
The walls were repaired, and for their speedy work they
gave God the praise.
And now Ezra stood upon the first pulpit of wood,
In sight of all the people, and taught them to be good;
And they bowed their faces to the ground and worshiped.
"And Ezra blessed the Lord the great God, and all the
people answered, Amen, Amen."

NOW, four hundred and sixty-two years before Christ
the history of Esther began,
When Ahasuerus, king of Persia, conquered Babylon.
And on this account, he appoints a solemn rejoicing and
praise,
Which lasted an hundred and eighty days;
On the conclusion of which, he gave a great feast for
the princes and people for seven days.
Now Queen Vashti made a like feast in her apartments,
the Bible says,
And the king's heart being merry with wine, sends for
the queen to show off her beauty;
But Vashti refuses to go, for she does not consider that
to be her duty,
Though she should lose her royal crown and perhaps
her head.
When she refused to comply the king was angry, and
called his counsellors for advice, and they said,
For fear her example might be bad, the king should give
her royal place to another.
This advice pleased the king, and Vashti was removed
from him forever.
After this, throughout the whole empire orders were
given
That every province should gather together all the fair
virgins,
So the king might choose one to be queen in Vashti's
place.
Now there lived in Shushan a Jew, Mordecai, a porter
of the royal palace.
Mordecai was one of those who had been carried captive
to Babylon,
And he having no children of his own,
Did bring up Esther, his Uncle Hadassah's daughter,
And she loved him as a father, for he had adopted her.
Now, this young woman was chosen queen, for she was
beautiful, and the fairest of the fair.
The king was delighted, and placed the royal crown up-
on her lovely head of hair.
Now, there was one Haman, the chief favorite of the
king,
And all the king's servants were to bow to him;
But Mordecai refused; perhaps he thought to bow to him

Was idolatrous adoration, and therefore a sin.

But this made Haman very angry, and so he and the
    king's scribes write a decree,

In which they declare that all the Jews are injurious to
    the nation,

And ask that both old and young should be slain.

They take it to the king on a certain day, and he gives
    permission to Haman to do as he wishes.

When Mordecai heard this, his lamentations were great.

He put on sackcloth and sat mournful at the king's gate.

The king had listened to Haman when he said the Jews'
    laws were diverse,

And that they did things that no other people did on the
    face of the earth.

And when Esther heard of Mordecai's grief, she sends
    to know what the matter could be,

Whereon he acquaints her by sending her a copy of the
    decree;

And tells her to go in unto the king and make suppli-
    cation for the Jews.

But Esther was at first afraid, knowing for this act he
    could kill her if he choose.

Then Mordecai tells her if she any love for her nation or
    father's house still did cherish,

She must now plead for her people or they all would
    perish.

Then she resolved to go, but first Mordecai and all the
    Jews will fast three days,

For if she gains the king's favor she will give to God
    the praise.

Now Esther puts on her royal apparel and goes to see
    if the king will accept her,

And to let her know she was welcome, he held out his
    golden sceptre.

And when the king asked her what she wanted him to
    do,

Esther requests him to come to a banquet, and bring
    Haman too.

And while they are at the banquet, the king desires her
    to make known her request;

But she invited them to come again the next day; and
    to please the king she tries her best.

Now, Haman was greatly puffed up, but on his return
    from the palace,

Mordecai again refused to bow; and now Haman's friends
 advise him to erect a gallows,
And to have Mordecai hanged thereon; but the same day
 Mordecai finds favor in the king's sight,
By the king finding an account of a conspiracy to take
 his life
That had been discovered by Mordecai, but until then
 the king never knew.
And when he inquires who saved him, it is told him
 that it was Mordecai the Jew.
Then he sends for Haman and asks, unto the man in
 whom the king delighteth what shall I do?
Haman thinking it was himself, said, put on the royal
 apparel and the crown too,
And upon the king's horse let him ride through the
 streets,
And proclaim that this man the king wants to honor to
 every one they meet.
But hark now! the king says, Mordecai is the man.
Haman in sorrow returned to his house; this disappoint-
 ment, how can he stand.
While he is lamenting to his friends, the queen sends
 him another banquet invitation.
When the king and Haman sit down, Esther gives her
 petition.
She prays the king that her life and her people's lives
 he would spare,
For a design was laid for their destruction, and she did
 not know how they would fare.
When the king asked in anger who it was that dared do
 this thing,
Esther, pointing to Haman, said he was the author of
 this sin,
And the king arose, called in servants who covered Ha-
 man's face,
And he was hanged on the gallows in Mordecai's place.

AFTER Esther, we come to the book of Job, supposed
to have been written by Solomon,
But by some thought to be more like Moses' songs.
Job was from the land of Uz, and was a perfect man and
upright.
He feared God and did all that was good in His sight.
And Job was very wealthy, and was considered the
greatest man in the east.
He had seven sons and three daughters, and an over
plenty of every kind of beast.
And Satan, then as now, went about like a roaring lion
seeking whom he might devour;
And the Lord said, consider my servant Job, over him
thou canst have no power;
And Satan answered, "Doth Job serve God for nought?"
Every thing that a man could desire he has got.
Take his wealth from him, and he will curse thee to thy
face.
And the Lord said, all that he hath is in thy power, only
to his person show grace.
So one after another came and told Job of the great de-
struction, yet he did not sin.
He said, "The Lord gave and the Lord hath taken
away; blessed be the name of the Lord."
Satan was disappointed; he found a man who, in afflic-
tion, loved, not abhorred.
Now, perhaps a year after this, Satan comes again to re-
new the strife,
And saith unto the Lord, "All that a man hath will he
give for his life;"
"But touch his bones and his flesh, and he will curse
thee."
And the Lord said, "Behold, he is in thine hand, only
save his life; but now see,
Satan smote him with sore boils from the sole of his foot
to the crown of his head;
And he scraped himself, having an intolerable itching,
and sat on an ash pile for a bed.
Now his wife gets out of patience, and tells him to curse
God and die.
"Thou speakest as one of the foolish women," was his
reply—
Like those who have no knowledge of God, of religion,
or of a future state.

Now, Satan was sifting Job like wheat, but his faith
    helped him to patiently wait.
Job has three friends, who come to comfort him, the Bi-
    ble says,
And they sat down upon the ground with him seven
    days;
And they saw his grief was great, but not a word was
    spoken whilst sitting on the earth.
Job himself first broke the silence by lamenting the day
    of his birth.
He longeth for death, but it cometh not;
He seeketh even more for death
    Than hid treasures are by some sought.
Now, those who came as comforters, upbraided him and
    said he was not patient enough;
But God to him was all in all; he cared not for their
    wicked taunts.
Those friends thought Job was suffering under a strange
    display of divine providence,
And that God was punishing him for some sin, and in
    him had no confidence.
Then the Lord said, "Gird up now thy loins like a man,
    for I will demand of thee,
And answer thou me.
Job having heard the Almighty's speech, acknowledges
    that his power is unlimited,
And that his wisdom is infinite.
But at last Job's sorrows came to a happy end;
But not until he had made intercession for his three
    friends.
So the Lord blessed the latter end of Job more than his
    beginning.
It was well for Job that he could suffer so much without
    sinning.
And the Lord now gave him thousands of sheep, camels
    and oxen,
Besides seven sons and three daughters, the loveliest
    and fairest of the land.
After this, Job lived an hundred and forty years,
Then died, being old and full of days.

THE prophet Jonah now by the word of the Lord was
  told to arise,
And go to Nineveh, for the wickedness of that city unto
  him cries;
But Jonah is afraid and tries to flee from the presence of
  the Lord,—
Went down to Joppa, found there a ship going to Tarsh-
  ish, and went aboard.
But they were overtaken by a storm, which appeared to
  have been sent by God;
But the mariners were afraid, and each of them cried
  unto his God.
But Jonah was lying down, and they said unto him, "O
  sleeper, arise,
Call upon thy God" for we fear we shall all perish.
Then they cast lots that they might know for whose
  cause this evil was upon them;
And Jonah was faithful, and said that he feared the
  Lord, although he had refused to obey him.
And the lot fell upon Jonah, and they said, "What shall
  we do unto thee?"
And he said, "Take me up and cast me into the sea;"
And they did, and the sea became calm again.
Then the men feared the Lord and offered a sacrifice.
And there appeared a great fish, which swallowed Jonah.
And in its belly Jonah lived three days and nights;
And Jonah prayed unto the Lord his God, whilst he was
  in the whale;
Then God caused the fish to sicken and it vomited him
  upon the dry land.

NOW we will write a verse from the last book of the
  Old Testament:
"But unto you that fear my name shall the Sun of right-
  eousness arise;" Christ is meant.
Now, he that is thirsty, need thirst no more,
For the waters of life are free evermore.
He shall supply the poor and needy,—
Ho! every one come without money;
Justice and mercy has offered this
Upon easy terms, receive, accept, embrace.

Oh! for you and me what wonderful grace:
A tried stone, a foundation sure,
A burden-bearer divinely pure;
One that has compassion when we're out of the way,
And a heart to bring us back when we go astray,
One that can pardon without upbraiding.
Come, oh then! all ye heavy ladened;
But come with faith to believe his word.
It will give comfort amidst our fears.
Faith like Abraham's, which taught him to say,
Yea, I will obey, though my son I must slay.
Then God was brief, and came with relief,
And saved him from this terrible grief.
By faith Gideon, with three hundred men,
Could do more than twelve tribes then.
And then there is David, Moses and Daniel;
Let us like them embrace the true Emanuel,
Come to him in prayer; he can turn darkness into glory,
And all our sorrow into song.
Go to him in all our grief and trouble;
What we ask, he will more than double.
When we think of the duties left undone,
It is time to heed his voice and to him come;
For with all this load of guilt and sin,
We have no peace without, within;
Tossing around like the restless waves,
Shut up under the law, and ready to perish,
How much we have to be thankful for,
How we ought to praise God and him adore.
Oh! blessed condition, we're ready to shout.
Jesus Christ says, "I will in no wise cast out."
Immediately upon Adam's sin,
The door of communion with God was shut in.
It was Jesus, the Mediator, that opened the door again,
And through him we have boldness and access, it is plain.
We can now come to God by a new and living way,
Consecrated for us through the veil—his flesh, that is to
    say.
Jesus Christ is fairer than the children of men;
The chiefest among ten thousand, then.
As the apple tree among the trees of the wood,
From him do bud forth the fruits that for all seasons and
    conditions are good,—

This Redeemer, who did not think it too much to sweat
  blood and die for men;
And shall we think it too much to watch, study, preach
  and pray, then?
The foxes have holes, and the birds of the air have nests,
But the Son of Man hath no place for his head to rest.
He was a man of sorrows and acquainted with grief;
Yet for our sake, he submitted voluntarily, and wants
  no relief,
" For God so loved the world that he gave his only be-
  gotten Son."
Christ answers, " Lo! I come, I delight to do thy will,"
  for we are one.
God's giving Christ implies a parting, delivering him
  into the hands of justice; oh, what a loss!
Let us consider to what he gave him,—even to death,
  and that of the cross.
Now we are redeemed with the precious blood of this
  Lamb,
And cleansed from all sin, by God's grace we shall stand
Free from the curse of the law, he being made a curse
  for us,
That we may receive the adoption of sons, who are but
  worms of the dust.
  Now, when Jesus knew he was only to be with his
  friends for a short time,
And whilst he was talking and telling them this,
  They had the Lord's Supper, when he blessed the
  bread and the wine;
And he said, " Take eat, this is my body which was
  broken for you.
This do in remembrance of me." This was intended for
  the whole world, too.
Now, when in the garden, the supper being finished,
He was betrayed by the Judas kiss;
And Pilate giving consent that it should be as they re-
  quired,
Jesus being delivered by the determinate counsel, soon
  expired.

THE Old and New Testaments, as to the spiritualness
of the worship, are the same,
Only the old was clouded with shadows, whilst the new
with Jesus our Saviour is plain;
And to see how near some passages are alike, let us com-
pare Exodus 25 and 40, what Moses heard on the
Mount,
With Hebrews 8 and 5. The language there is the same,
about.
The Lord has made the new covenant with the house of
Judah.
The first covenant is now old and ready to vanish away.
In the fullness of time, a sign of the good tidings to
the shepherds was given;
The angels sang, and at Bethlehem the babe in a manger
was lain.
Now Herod, the king, feared a rival to the throne,
And he sent magicians that the child's age might be
known.
And that he may destroy Jesus, he gives orders that the
babes of two years and under must all be slain;
But God frustrates his purpose by telling Joseph to get
into Egypt with Jesus and his mother, saying,
Stay until he should hear from him again.
After Herod's death, they back to Nazareth, their old
residence, went,
Where we find him, a child of twelve years, and where
his childhood is spent.
Now, as a pupil, he is permitted to ask questions of the
old Jewish teachers of the law,
And the old Doctors wonder at the child for what they
heard and saw.
After awhile we read of John the Baptist, the forerunner
of Christ, appearing among men,
And announcing the kingdom of heaven at hand then.
John the Baptist preached in the wilderness of repent-
ance for the remission of sins,
And about this time, Jesus went and was baptized of
him.
Then we read of Jesus being tempted of the devil forty
days and nights,
The devil offering him great things, and showing him
beautiful sights.

And after his temptation, we read of his many miracles,
  which we will not be able to tell in this little book;
But will tell you where you may find them,—on the last
  page, if you will look.
The Saviour called twelve Apostles to preach,
The lost sheep of the house of Israel they were to teach.
Of those disciples, John was the loved one who leaned
  on the Saviour's breast,
And in so doing, acknowledged that there only was per-
  fect rest;
And Jesus on him could truly rely;
Jesus showed this by telling him to care for his aged
  mother when he was about to die.
The history of Thomas is rather brief.
He is noted most for his unbelief,—
Would not believe Jesus had risen until he could see his
  hands and side.
When permitted to see, cries, "My Lord and my God,"
  with mouth opened wide.
Peter, who made the great confession of Christ's Messiah-
  ship,
Upon the rock of whose faith we must all worship.
Then there was Andrew, James, Philip, Bartholomew
  and Matthew,
Another James, Thaddeus, Simon, and Judas the trai-
  tor.

————

Now, dear children, I bid you an affectionate adieu,
And hope you may search the Scriptures to see if what
  I have written is true.
May they be your guide; may you on the Saviour re-
  cline,
Choose him for your friend now, and for all future time.

The following classification of our Saviour's miracles, may be found convenient and useful:*

I. THOSE WHICH RELATE TO HUMAN SUSTENANCE.

Miracle.	Place.	Record.
Water turned into Wine,	Cana,	John ii, 5-11.
Two draughts of Fishes,	See of Galilee	{ Luke v, 1-11. John xxi, 1-14.
Five thousand fed,	Decapolis,	Matt. xiv, 15-21
Four thousand fed,	Decapolis,	Matt. xv, 32-39.

II. THOSE WHICH RELATE TO HIS CURING DISEASES.

The nobleman's son,	Cana,	John iv, 46-54.
Peter's wife's mother,	Caper'm,	Mark i, 30-31.
A centurion's servant,	Caper'm,	Matt. viii, 5-13.
Diseased cripple at Bethesda,	Jerusalem,	John v, 1–9.
Canaanite's daughter,	Near Tyre,	Matt. xv, 22-28.

The pathetic expostulation of this woman has not its equal in the Gospel history.

III. THOSE WHICH RELATE TO CURES PERFORMED ON DEMONIACS.

An unclean spirit,	Caper'm,	Mark i, 23-26.
The two from the tombs,	Gadara,	Matt. viii, 28-34.
The dumb demoniac,	Caper'm,	Matt. ix, 32.
The blind and dumb,	Caper'm,	Matt. xii, 22.
The boy cured,	Tabor,	Matt. xvii, 18.

IV. THOSE WHICH RELATE TO THE REMOVAL OF VARIOUS INFIRMITIES.

Sight restored to two men,	Caper'm,	Matt. ix, 29.
A withered hand cured,	Judea,	Matt. xii, 10.
Man deaf and dumb cured,	Decapolis,	Mark vii, 31.
Blind man cured,	Bethesda,	Mark viii, 22.
Man born blind cured,	Jerusalem,	John ix.
Two restored to sight,	Jericho,	Matt. xx, 30.
The ear of Malchus healed,	Gethsem.,	Luke xxii, 50.
Man sick of the palsy cured,	Caper'm,	Matt. ix, 1-8.
Leper healed,	Caper'm,	Mark i, 40-45.
Ten lepers cleansed,	Samaria,	Luke xvii, 11-19

V. MIRACLES UPON INANIMATE SUBJECTS.

Tempest calmed,	Sea Gal.,	Matt. viii, 23-27.
Money found in fishe's mouth	Do.	Matt. xvii, 27.
Walking on the sea,	Do.	Matt. xiv, 25.
Blasting of the fig tree,	Olivet,	Matt. xxi, 18.

VI. THOSE WHICH EXHIBIT HIS POWER TO RAISE THE DEAD.

Widow's son,	Nain,	Luke vii, 11-17.
Jairus' daughter,	Caper'm,	Matt. ix, 18-25.
Lazarus,	Bethany,	John xi.

*Covel's Dictionary of the Bible.